CHURCH CHOIR WARM-UPS
FOR VOICE, BODY & ...

Compiled, Written and Adapted by Janet ...

T0080175

 Indicates track number on enclosed CD

HAL•LEONARD® CORPORATION

7777 W. BLUEMOUND RD. P.O. BOX 13819 MILWAUKEE, WI 53213

Copyright © 2013 by HAL LEONARD CORPORATION
International Copyright Secured   All Rights Reserved
www.halleonard.com

In Australia Contact:
Hal Leonard Australia Pty. Ltd.
4 Lentara Court
Cheltenham, Victoria, 3192 Australia
Email: ausadmin@halleonard.com.au

PREFACE

I became a church organist before I could legally drive. In my small farming community in North Dakota, it was simply understood that if you could play the piano and the church needed your help, you stepped up. So my piano teacher placed me on the organ bench when I was 13 years old, and my feet could not yet touch the pedals. So she patiently taught me how to "crawl" from chord to chord, explained the functions of the different stops, and told me to skip the pedals until I could reach them comfortably. We managed to pull it off and almost 40 years later, I'm still at it. My role as a church musician is as varied as the churches I have served—organist, adult choir director, youth choir director, bell choir director, praise band leader, and director of music at many different churches of many different denominations. After all these years, I still believe that there is no better way to use the talents that God has given me than to serve in music ministry. Even when I'm bone tired as I arrive at church for three hours of rehearsal after a full day of work, I am always refreshed and revitalized when I leave. What could be better than spending an evening with good people, making music for the glory of God and sharing a laugh or two?

Over the years, I have studied and researched music and resources to help me guide volunteer musicians into confident singers and players. I haven't yet come across a resource like the one you hold in your hands—a choral warm-up book designed especially for churches. Some of these exercises are adapted from previous warm-ups I have used, and some are newly composed just for this book. My hope is that this collection will allow your church choir to grow in voice, body and soul. May your music ministry be blessed with committed volunteers, a full tenor section and at least one soprano that can sustain a high G!

To the glory of God,

Janet Day

HOW TO USE THIS BOOK

The flexible set-up of this book allows you to use this resource in a variety of ways:

- Use for large group (choir), small group (ensembles), or individual (solo) warm-ups.

- Choose an exercise from each chapter every rehearsal or,

- Choose exercises that focus on the needs of your choir or singer(s) or,

- Choose the exercises that concentrate on the needs of a particular piece of music.

- The original purchaser of this book has permission to reproduce any of the singer music exercises for church or educational use. Many of the exercises may be taught by rote, but for some of the four-part exercises and the sight-singing materials, you may choose to project them (see next bullet point) or reproduce for each singer.

- Singer parts for each music exercise are included on the enhanced audio CD included with this book. Each PDF (portable document format) file can be projected on a large screen for whole group viewing, reproduced for individual singers or imported into your Interactive Whiteboard application for your own unique use. These files are the property of the original purchaser of this book and cannot be transferred to another person or organization. To access the PDF files from a PC, click on My Computer, then right click on the drive in which you placed the CD. Click Open. You should then see a folder named "PDF files." Mac users will see two icons on the desktop: "Audio CD" and "PDF files."

- Note there are no dynamics or tempo markings throughout the music exercises. The director should choose the tempo that works best for the group or individual. Vary the dynamics. The enclosed demonstration CD should serve merely as a guide.

- The enclosed demonstration CD can be used for a "hands-free" warm-up, a member-directed warm-up, or a transportable warm-up for off-site rehearsals and services. The track numbers are indicated throughout.

- The accompaniments are meant to enhance the exercises. However, if you choose to modulate in a different direction than the accompaniment or for more repetitions than the accompaniment, feel free to sing the exercise a cappella or continue modulating upward or downward with your skilled accompanist.

However you choose to utilize this book, may it offer useful exercises and ideas to warm the voices, hearts, bodies and souls of each member of your choir.

—The Publisher

CHAPTER 1
PREPARE WITH PRAYER

Begin each rehearsal with a devotion or prayer.
Choose from one of the following or create your own.

SAINT THERESA'S PRAYER

May today there be peace within.
May you trust God that you are exactly where you are meant to be.
May you not forget the infinite possibilities that are born of faith.
May you use those gifts that you have received, and pass on the love that has been given to you.
May you be content knowing you are a child of God.
Let this presence settle into your bones, and allow your soul the freedom to sing, dance, praise and love.
It is there for each and every one of us.
Amen.

THE CHORISTERS' PRAYER

O Lord, be with us as we meet in Your name.
Open our minds to Your Spirit and
Grant that what we sing with our lips,
We may believe in our hearts,
And what we believe in our hearts,
We may show forth in our lives,
Through Jesus Christ, our Lord.
Amen.

PRAYER FOR ARTISTS AND MUSICIANS

O God, whom saints and angels delight to worship in heaven: Be ever present with your servants who seek through art and music to perfect the praises offered by your people on earth; and grant to them even now glimpses of your beauty, and make them worthy at length to behold it unveiled for evermore; through Jesus Christ our Lord.
Amen.
—From the Book of Common Prayer

PRAYER OF SAINT FRANCIS

Lord, make me an instrument of your peace.
Where there is hatred, let me sow love.
Where there is injury, pardon.
Where there is despair, hope.
Where there is darkness, light.
Where there is sadness, joy.
O Divine Master,
Grant that I may not so much seek to be consoled, as to console;
To be understood, as to understand;
To be loved, as to love.
For it is in giving that we receive.
It is in pardoning that we are pardoned,
And it is in dying that we are born to Eternal Life.
Amen.

THE CHURCH MUSICIANS' PRAYER

O God, you have blessed us with talents and gifts beyond our deserving. We come before You now in joyful response to Your blessings; to foster our talents and to offer their first fruits to You.

We ask that You strengthen our voices and bodies for Your service. Help us as we emphasize in song the same message our worship leaders express in words and prayers. Fill us with Your Holy Spirit and transform our music into a gift pleasing to You and meaningful to the congregation we serve. We ask all this in the name of Your Son, Jesus Christ.
Amen.

THE MUSICIANS' PRAYER

Oh Lord, please bless this music that it might glorify Your name. May the talent that You have bestowed upon us be used only to serve You. Let this music be a witness to Your majesty and love, and remind us that You are always watching, and listening, from Your throne above. May Your presence and beauty be found in every note, and may the words that are sung reach the hearts of Your people so they will draw closer to You. May Your Spirit guide us through every measure so that we might be the instruments of Your peace, and proclaim Your glory with glad voices.
Amen.

CHAPTER 2
BREATHE IN THE SPIRIT
Breathing Exercises

Breathing exercises not only prepare inner muscles to control the diaphragm, but they also supply well-needed oxygen to the brain after a long day of work and tension. An added bonus of breathing exercises is relaxation, quiet time and a gathered focus on the rehearsal. Choose one of the following for each rehearsal.

GOOD IN, BAD OUT

Establish a steady beat with handclaps, finger snaps or hand drum. Use these words to aid meditation and tranquility while breathing. Close your eyes and inhale for eight beats, SAY "Breathe in everything that is good—green grass, lilacs, a baby's smile, a shoe sale, etc."

While exhaling for eight beats, SAY "Breathe out everything that is bad—heavy traffic, headache, tension at work, an argument with a family member or friend, etc." Repeat using four counts, then two counts, using your inner muscles to control the rate of inhalation and exhalation.

RIBS RAISED, SHOULDERS RELAXED

Raise your arms overhead slowly while inhaling. Then exhale your air on "ss" while slowly lowering your arms to their original position. Try to maintain the raised rib cage while lowering your arms.

YAWN SIGH

Breathe in as if you are going to yawn, but instead exhale on a gentle vocal sigh from a high pitch descending to a low pitch, releasing vocal tension as you descend.

MILK SHAKE BREATHING

Imagine there is a milkshake as large as the sanctuary. Hold your arms out from your body as if you were holding this giant milkshake and "drink" the air through a giant "straw." Exhale on a yawn-sigh.

ELEVATOR PLATFORM

Imagine that there is an elevator platform at the bottom of your lungs. Drop the platform toward the floor as you inhale. Inhale four counts. Exhale on a whispered "ah." Repeat with five, then six counts.

WHAT IS THIS LOVELY FRAGANCE?

Bend at the waist and pick an imaginary flower. Inhale the "fragrance" while slowly standing up. Exhale on a yawn-sigh. Adapt as necessary for older singers who may feel uncomfortable bending over.

I AM A SANCTUARY

Inhale while raising your arms overhead (notice the expanded rib cage). Exhale on several short bursts of "ss" and ending in "sanctuary."

ss   ss   ss   ss   sanctuary (repeat 1 or 2 times on each breath)

SEE HOW HE SAVES

Place your fingertips at the bottom of your rib cage. As you inhale, notice the expansion of the rib cage. As you sing the following exercise, feel the movement in your diaphragm area.

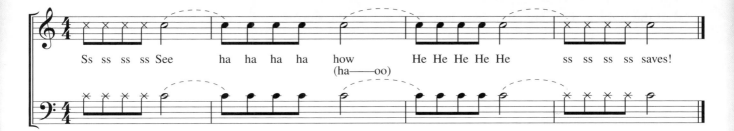

HYMN TO BREATHING

Choose a familiar hymn and speak the rhythms using an unvoiced consonant. Switch the consonant on each stanza. Place your fingertips just below your rib cage and feel the breathing muscles move. Here is an example using the hymn tune HYMN TO JOY.

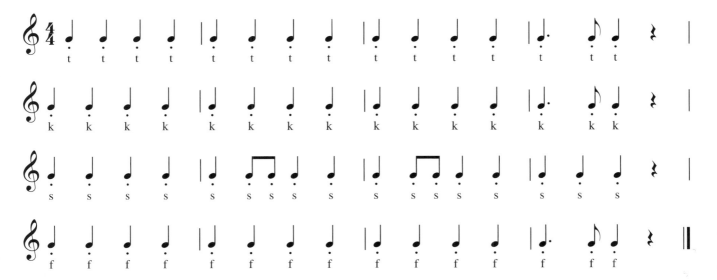

BALLOON DEMO

As a demonstration for the benefits of breath control, blow up a balloon and then quickly release the air. Your choir will see it fly around the room as the air quickly empties. Next, blow up the balloon and then control the release of the air by holding the neck of the balloon. As singers, we can control the release of our air by practicing breath control. This will increase our air reserves and allow us to time the release so the entire musical phrase is supported.

CHAPTER 3
FEEL THE SPIRIT
Movement Exercises

After you've replenished your brain with oxygen from the breathing exercises, try these physical movements to warm-up your body. It is always a good feeling to stretch your neck, back and shoulder muscles after a long day. Choose a stretching activity from the list below or create your own.

SHOULDERS HIGH AND LOW
Lift the left shoulder high and let it fall. Repeat with the right shoulder and finally both shoulders.

RAG DOLL STRETCH
Stretch your arms over your head, and then fall forward like a rag doll. Slowly rise up, straightening one vertebra at a time until you are in a good standing posture. Stress to choir members to only stretch until your body says "stop" or stretch to the limit or edge. Be careful not to overstretch and pull a muscle or pinch a nerve. Listen to your body!

REACH TO THE HEAVENS
Stretch, with hands high overhead. In a normal standing position or seated tall, raise the right hand, palm up to the sky, then the left hand, palm up, then both. Feel the stretch along the sides of your body. Repeat.

CLASP AND PULL
In a standing position or seated tall, clasp hands in front and raise them above head. Use your left hand to pull the right hand over the top of your head, trying to keep your elbow as straight as possible. Switch sides, using your right hand to pull the left hand over the top of your head. Feel the stretch in your shoulder area.

HEAD ROCK AND ROLL
Rock/tilt your head slowly from side to side, trying to touch your ear lobe to your shoulder without raising your shoulder. Repeat several times. Next, rock/tilt your head to one side, then roll to the front, trying to touch your chin to your clavicle, then continue rolling to end in a tilt to the other side. Repeat several times. Next, try rolling to the back, repeating several times.

HUG THYSELF
With your right arm over your left, hug yourself by reaching your arms around you, trying to touch your shoulders blades with your opposite hands. That is, your right hand reaches around to touch your left shoulder blade, and your left hand reaches around to touch your right shoulder blade. Stay in the stretch for one minute, and then switch arms so your left arm is on top.

FEEL THE WARMING TOUCH

In a standing position, facing the director, all singers should turn to the left. Place the palms of your hands in the "safe" zone on the back of the singer in front of you. The "safe" zone is the area between the shoulder blades. Rub gentle circles in this area to warm up the muscles of the back. Do this for one minute. Face the director again. Then all singers should turn to the right and return the favor to the next singer.

SPIDER SENSATIONS

In the same manner as the above "warming touch" activity, instead of rubbing circles in the "safe" zone, make "spiders." Spiders are made by rolling the fingertips one by one from the little finger to the thumb, like drumming your fingers on a tabletop.

CLOCK STRETCHES

Stand tall and imagine a clock face is located about one foot behind you. Stretch your right hand high above your head and reach back to touch your palm on the "11" of the imaginary clock. Feel the stretch in the front of your shoulder. After stretching there for five to ten seconds, move your palm down to the "10" and so on. Stop your right side stretches at the "7." Switch to your left side, repeating the process starting on the "1" and so on down to the "5."

FEELING THE CROSS

Cross your right arm on top of the left arm meeting at the elbows. Bend your arms at the elbows, allowing fingertips to point upward. Gently pull your left arm toward your body, feeling the stretch in your right shoulder. Switch sides and repeat.

CHAPTER 4
IN A POSTURE OF PRAISE
Exercises to Promote Good Posture

POSTURE OF PRAISE

Stand with your feet apart as wide as your shoulders, with the right foot slightly forward. Keep the knees relaxed and unlocked. The chest should be high, the shoulders down, the arms and hands relaxed at your sides. The head should be erect, with the chin not raised. This is good singing posture. If your choir rehearses sitting down, encourage them to only bend at the hip and knee joints to sit. The upper portion of the body remains the same as if standing.

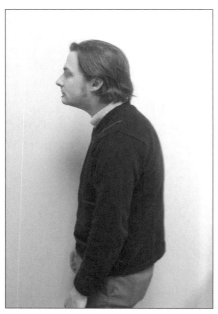

BAD POSTURE STANDING

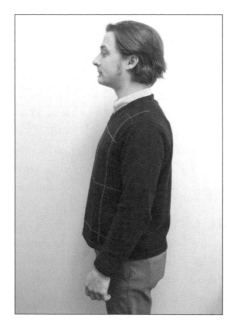

GOOD POSTURE STANDING

BAD POSTURE SEATED

GOOD POSTURE SEATED

STAND TALL AGAINST THE WALL

If your rehearsal space allows, have each singer stand tall with his/her back against a wall. Place one heel against the wall and the other heel comfortable away from the wall for balance. Take a moment to feel each part of the body that is touching the wall: heel, buttocks, shoulder blades, back of head. Now step away from the wall, keeping the same alignment. Do not lock your knees. Remember this stature as you prepare to sing.

BALANCE THE MUSIC

Balance a piece of choral music on the top of your head. Turn your head slowly to the left, return to center, and then repeat to the right. The head movements should be smooth with eyes ahead, chin level, head, neck and shoulders relaxed. Once you have achieved balance, hum or sing a well-known hymn tune. If body is in alignment, the music will remain in place. Don't let the music fall! Build up your posture strength to balance your entire choir folder on the top of your head.

THE TRIUNE BODY

Think of your body as being in three parts: the head, the torso and the legs. Each part is intertwined so what we do with one will affect another. That is, if we are out of alignment, a part of our body will need to make up for that alignment and "carry the load" for the part that has shifted. When standing tall, check the following:

    a. Feet should be firmly planted under your torso and weight is balanced on both feet.

    b. Knees are soft, never locked to a straight position.

    c. Lengthen your spine by pulling your tailbone down and your head up.

    d. Balance your head on top of the spine so that the neck and jaw muscles are free and feel loose.

When moving to a seated position, simply bend at the knees and the hips. The upper portion of the body remains in alignment.

TIP TOE TO GOOD POSTURE

Relax and take off your shoes. Stand with your feet flat, arms to your side, palms facing forward. Rise slowly up on to the tip of your toes and feel your back slightly arch and your shoulders move back to help you keep your balance. Try to retain this feeling as you gently lower yourself back down to your heels. This is proper singing posture.

PINCH IS A CINCH

Because most of us are inclined to slouch our shoulders forward, our back muscles may need strengthening to be more "accepting" of proper posture. To retrain these back and shoulder muscles, try this. Get in the proper singing posture described above. Then in a seated or standing position, "pinch" your shoulder blades together in a downward motion as though you were trying to hold a tennis ball between your shoulder blades. Hold this position for 3–5 seconds, and then relax. Repeat.

WE ARE CLIMBING JACOB'S LADDER

Have singers flop over from the waist like a rag doll. Arms should be freely swinging and relaxed. They should imagine their spines to be like Jacob's ladder. They must place one rung on top of the other as they slowly bring their bodies up to a standing position. Lastly, set the head on the top of Jacob's ladder.

CHAPTER 5
LET YOUR VOICES SING PRAISE
Vocal Exercises

After your mind and your body are prepared, it is now time to warm-up the singing voice. As most church choirs rehearse in the evening, singers have already been using their speaking voice throughout the day. The goal of these vocal exercises is to have singers "switch" into their singing voice. On Sunday mornings, however, these vocal warm-ups may very well be one of the first sounds uttered by the singers. Use them to activate the vocal muscles. Choose one or two of the exercises from the group below.

PRAISE GOD

Breathe in with the lips in an "oo" shape, and then sing the following exercise. Repeat the pattern at different pitch levels, both higher and lower.

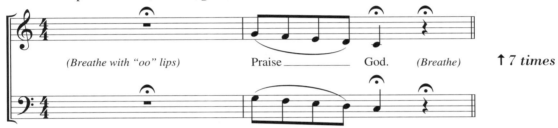

Piano Accompaniment • Page 31

YAHWEH

To focus on the "ah" and "eh" vowel sounds, sing the following exercise with a relaxed jaw. Hold the last note and listen for a full, blended choral sound that is in tune with the other voices around you.

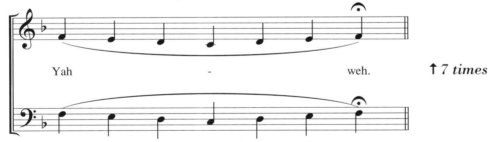

Piano Accompaniment • Page 32

ALLELUIA, MANY VOICES AS ONE

Change smoothly from one vowel to the next as you practice the descending scale. Take an expanded ribcage breath and try to sing the entire pattern on one breath. Keep a relaxed jaw and vertical space inside the mouth. Listen to your neighbors on all sides to be sure you are matching your vowel sounds, tone quality, dynamic level and tempo with those around you.

Piano Accompaniment • Page 33

HALLELUJAH VOWELS

Sing this exercise to practice the five basic vowels.

AH   EH   EE   OH   OO

Hah	hah	hah	hah	leh	eh	eh	eh	loo	oo	oo	oo	yah.
Hee	hee	hee	hee	noh	oh	oh	ohs	yoo	oo	oo	oo	oo.
Hee	hee	hee	hee	noh	oh	oh	ohs	mee	ee	ee	ee	too.
Hoh	hoh	hoh	hoh	sah	ah	ah	ah	nah	ah	ah	ah	ah.

↑ *3 times*

1. Hallelujah.   2. He knows you.   3. He knows me too.   4. Hosanna.

Piano Accompaniment • Page 36

LET US SING A SONG OF JOY

Concentrate on the pure vowel sound of the word "joy." Activate the diaphragm muscle on the staccato notes.

Joy, joy, joy, joy, joy, joy. Let__ us__ sing__ a__ song of joy.

↑ *7 times*

Piano Accompaniment • Page 37

GOD LOVES YOU

Concentrate on the pure vowel sounds of the words (eh-oo, oo-ee, ah-oo). Activate the breathing muscle on the staccato notes. Open the "oo" to "oh" on the higher notes.

Hey you! Who me? God loves you - hoo!

↑ *7 times*

Piano Accompaniment • Page 40

HOSANNA

Sing the following exercise as if you were calling to a friend or shouting praises to God. This helps develop an open throat and free tone.

Ho - san - na,

↑ *5 times*

Piano Accompaniment • Page 42

SING WITH RESONANCE

Resonance comes from the Latin word *resonare* that means to resound. In singing, the sound that comes from the vibrating vocal cords is not audible until it is amplified by coming into contact with the bony regions of the body and face. This amplification develops and increases the sound.

In the following exercise, sing the word "sing" and immediately close to the "ng" sound. You will notice that the sound is very nasal and small. On cue from the director, open the "ng" to "ah" and notice what happens in your mouth. Feel your throat "opening" into a fuller sound. This movement is call "raising the soft palate," and helps give the voice resonance.

Sing(ng) Ah,   ↑ *7 times*

Piano Accompaniment • Page 43

RING THE BELLS

This exercise helps to develop resonance in the tone. Sing lightly and without effort. Keep your facial muscles relaxed. Close immediately to the "ng" on every half note.

Ring the bells of Christ-mas ring - a ding   ↓ *8 times*

Piano Accompaniment • Page 44

CHAPTER 6
LET US GROW IN THE LORD
Exercises to Increase Vocal Flexibility and Range

Increase your vocal flexibility and range by choosing one of the following exercises each rehearsal.

SING, SING, SING

Singers are often required to sing long phrases consisting of legato melismas. Good breath support and vowel repetition will help you sing these passages rhythmically and well in tune. As you sing the following exercise, concentrate on "repeating the vowel" in the eighth note melismas.

Piano Accompaniment • Page 46

SING ALLELUIA

Sing the following exercise with a slight diaphragm push on each downbeat. As you sing the slurred passage, think of repeating the vowel and don't allow and "h" to separate the different notes.

Piano Accompaniment • Page 49

I KNOW THAT MY REDEEMER LIVES

The singing voice can be divided into three basic regions, called registers. These registers are often identified as chest (low), middle, and head (high) registers. By working consistently on the breath, forming correct vowels, and producing a good tone, a singer can unify these registers to produce a smooth, natural-sounding voice. Sing the following exercise keeping a uniform sound between registers.

JOB 19:25

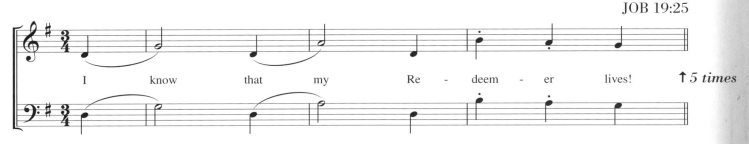

Piano Accompaniment • Page 51

HALLELUJAH, CHRIST HAS ARISEN

Activate your diaphragm muscle as you sing the accented notes in this exercise that will increase vocal flexibility and range. Sing at a slower tempo at first until you can be absolutely accurate. You'll need good breath support to sing each four-bar phrase in one breath.

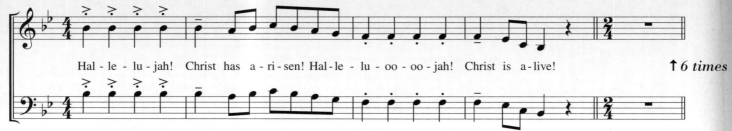

Piano Accompaniment • Page 53

GOD IS GOOD

Even though this next exercise is spirited and lively, remember to create a tall vowel on each word clipping it off with a short, crisp consonant, and then moving to the next tall vowel. Use your diaphragm to accentuate the accented notes and staccato notes. Listen carefully so that the men's voices balance the women's voices.

Piano Accompaniment • Page 56

FOR UNTO US ARPEGGIOS

Use the following exercise on arpeggios to activate your diaphragm, increase vocal range, and tune your part with other sections as you cadence in four parts.

Piano Accompaniment • Page 58

CHAPTER 7
SING GOD'S WORDS CLEARLY
Exercises to Develop Diction Skills and Proper Vowel Placement

Spreading the Word through music requires good articulation and diction so that all may hear the message clearly. Use these exercises to develop the articulators — the teeth, the lips, and the tongue — while maintaining a tall vowel sound.

I'LL SHOUT IT

Sing this phrase with good articulation. Be careful not to distort the vertical vowel sound of each word.

I'll shout it from the top of the moun-tain; The Lord is good, let us praise His name! ↑ *5 times*

Piano Accompaniment • Page 61

In the next exercises, remember to:

- Maintain a good singing posture.
- Take a full, expanded rib cage breath before each repetition.
- Activate the articulators (lips, teeth, tongue) to articulate all the consonants so they are clear and precise.
- Produce good tone by concentrating on pure vowel formation and vertical space inside the mouth.
- Sing both consonant and vowels with the same breath support.

MUSIC, SWEET MUSIC

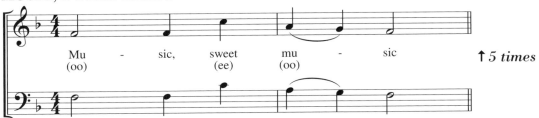

Mu - sic, sweet mu - sic
(oo) (ee) (oo)   ↑ *5 times*

Piano Accompaniment • Page 63

AND THE NIGHT

And the night shall be filled with mu - sic.
(ah) (ee) (oo)   ↑ *5 times*

Piano Accompaniment • Page 64

OLD NOAH'S BOAT FLOATS

Concentrate on singing with a tall open "oh" vowel.

Piano Accompaniment • Page 66

BRING A GIFT OF SILK TO THE KING

Practice the vowel sound "i" as in bring, gift, silk and King.

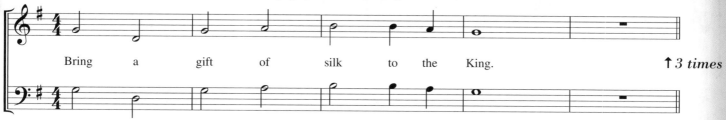

Piano Accompaniment • Page 68

ONE GOD, MANY MEMBERS

Practice the vowel sounds "ah," "eh," and "ee" with a lifted palate. Remain on the tall vowel as long as possible until cutting off the sound with the consonant that follows. Then quickly move to the next tall vowel sound.

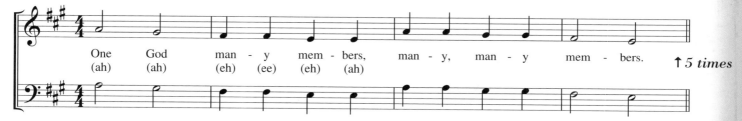

Piano Accompaniment • Page 70

SINGING THE CONSONANT "R"

There are two kinds of "r" sounds that are used when singing in English. The American "r" is the "r" that is used in daily speech. The flipped "r" could be described by the saying "very good" sounding as "veddy good" like they say it in England (the tip of the tongue at the back of the front teeth). Both are used in singing.

In singing, we must carefully prepare the articulation of words containing the "r" sound. This is because an "r" can affect the vowel sound that it precedes or follows. Say or sing the word "care" on a unison pitch, holding the vowel and gradually change to the "r" sound (kehrrrrrr_____). Did you notice the movement of the tongue and the change in the sound?

Tips:

- Whether you choose to sing an American "r" or a flipped "r" will depend on the kind of music you are singing. Study professional recordings of the piece or research its history to find out what is appropriate. It is important, however, for an ensemble to have a uniform sound on an "r," since even one or two voices can affect the sound and intonation of the entire group.

- Never sing "r"s before consonant sounds. For example: "The Lord is my shepherd" would be sung "The Lahd is my shephahd."

- Never sing the "r" before a rest or if it occurs on the last word of the song. For example: "And I will dwell in the house of the Lord forever" would be sung "And I will dwell in the house of the Lahd forevah."

- Always sing the "r" before a vowel, whether flipped or not. This holds true whether the "r" is in the same word with the vowel or in adjoining words.

REJOICE!

Practice the following exercise using first the American "r" and then the flipped "r."

Piano Accompaniment • Page 72

CHRIST STAR WE SEE TONIGHT

RULE: De-emphasize "r" before a consonant: This can be a challenging concept for novice or volunteer choir members, but a necessary one in gaining a pleasing choral tone quality. There are some exceptions to this practice, mostly in pop music, but in general, this rule applies. Practice the following examples, omitting the "r" sound when it precedes a consonant.

Piano Accompaniment • Page 73

CHRIST STAR MERGING

In the following exercise, the ending "st" sound of "Christ" and the beginning "st" sound of "star" should merge together to form one sound to maintain a smooth legato phrase.

Piano Accompaniment • Page 74

WHAT'S WRONG WITH MY DIPHTHONG?

A diphthong consists of two "vowel sounds" – the primary vowel sound and a secondary vowel sound. This secondary vowel sound is (usually) at the very end of the diphthong, just before the final consonant or next word or syllable. As you sing each word, concentrate on maintaining the pure, primary vowel sound. Just as you release, place the final secondary vowel sound at the end of the tone. It should be very understated and unstressed.

Repeat with:

why	[(oo)ah—(ee)]
time	[(t)ah—(eem)]
joy	[(j)oh—(ee)]
though	[(th)oh—(oo)]
day	[(d)eh—(ee)]
now	[(n)ah—(oo)]

↓6 times

Piano Accompaniment • Page 77

SOFT STILLNESS

Never prolong the "s" into a hiss. Move quickly to the next vowel or consonant.

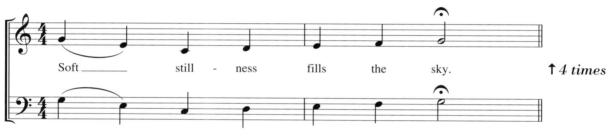

↑ 4 times

Piano Accompaniment • Page 78

I CAN DO ALL THINGS THROUGH CHRIST

Sing this next exercise with crisp clean consonants and tall open vowels. Activate your diaphragm muscles on the accented notes.

PHILIPPIANS 4:13

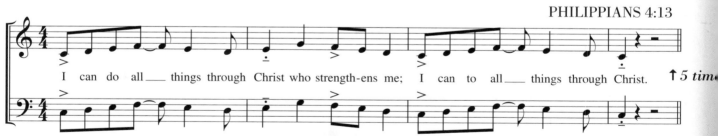

↑ 5 times

Piano Accompaniment • Page 79

CHAPTER 8
WE ARE ALL ONE IN CHRIST
Exercises for Choral Blend, Balance and Intonation

Singing in a choir requires great listening ears from all members to sing in tune and blend as a whole group — much different than singing a solo. Use the following exercises to develop keen listening habits and good choral blend.

PRAISE HIM

Practice the following exercise concentrating on a free, relaxed and unforced tone. Listen to your neighbors and carefully tune the chords in the last two measures.

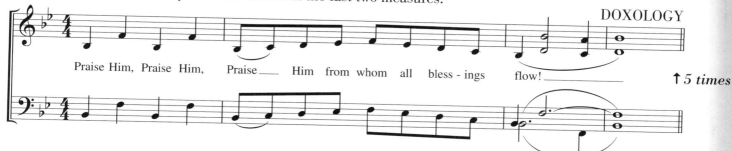

Piano Accompaniment • Page 81

SING PRAISE

Close immediately to the "ng" on "sing" at the beginning of this exercise to develop resonance or ring to the tone. On the descending passage, listen to your neighbors to tune the dissonant notes, as well as the resolution of that dissonance.

Piano Accompaniment • Page 83

ALLELUIA, AMEN

Treat each eighth note as a fermata in the second measure. As each pitch moves, listen to your neighbors to tune the dissonant notes. Identify by section which two notes are dissonant. The identified section should bring out the two dissonant notes and relax the sound as it resolves. Listen to the blend and the balance between moving parts.

Al - le - lu - ia, Al - le - lu - ia, A - men.

Piano Accompaniment • Page 84

ALLELUIA

Most hymns are homophonic, meaning all parts (Soprano, Alto, Tenor, Bass) move together in harmony creating chords. Sing this next exercise listening to all parts so that everyone moves together to the next chord at the same time, the sound is balanced between sections and each vowel is tall and matches all other singers.

Al - le - lu - ia, Al - le - lu - ia.   ↑ *5 times*

Piano Accompaniment • Page 85

THE LORD IS MY SHEPHERD

In most cases, drop your jaw for upward leaps and increase your breath support. For downward leaps, close your lips slightly and sing lighter.

PSALM 23

The Lord Is my Shep - herd and I shall not want.   ↑ *5 times*

Piano Accompaniment • Page 88

LOVE IS PATIENT

Practice open vowels with slurred notes. Make sure you hold on to the open vowel sound until the very last moment when you clip on the consonant and move to the next open vowel. This exercise allows for practice in legato singing, and also ascending and descending thirds. Note unison vs. part-singing between men and women's voices.

1 CORINTHIANS 13:4

Love is pa - tient, love is kind.

↑ *5 times*

Piano Accompaniment • Page 90

WHERE TWO OR MORE ARE GATHERED

Rounds are terrific ways to build independence in singers and balance between sections. You can use the following rounds in a number of ways:

1. Split group into two sections, Section 1 begins, and Section 2 starts when Section 1 reaches circle 2.
2. Split group into three sections, Section 1 begins, and Section 2 starts when Section 1 reaches circle 2, Section 3 starts when Section 1 reaches circle 3.

Vary your groups each time you sing the round. Divide into men vs. women, high voices vs. low voices, Sopranos, Altos, and Men, etc.

MATTHEW 18:20
Music: Music Alone Shall Live

Where two or more are gath - ered, I'm there.

Where two or more are, Where two or more are,

Where two or more are gath - ered, I'm there.

Piano Accompaniment • Page 92

CHURCH CHOIR WARM-UPS

A ROUND OF AMENS

To practice intonation and blend in a minor key, first sing the following exercise in unison. Then, sing the exercise as a round with Voice 1 holding the last pitch until all voices have reached a unison pitch for tuning. Repeat at different pitch levels, if desired.

↑ 2 times

Piano Accompaniment • Page 94

LET'S SING FOR JOY UNTO THE LORD

In this four-part round, split group into four sections. Section 1 begins, Section 2 starts when Section 1 reaches circle 2, Section 3 starts when Section 1 reaches circle 3, and Section 4 starts when Section 1 reaches circle 4. Vary your sections as before. Strive for balance between sections in vowel formation, dynamics, phrasing, etc.

PSALM 95:1
Music: Tallis' Canon

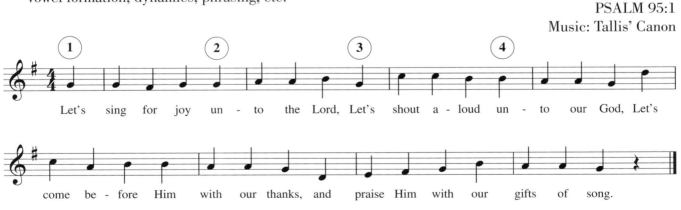

Piano Accompaniment • Page 97

CHAPTER 9
OPEN OUR EARS SO THAT WE MAY HEAR; OPEN OUR EYES SO THAT WE MAY SEE

Exercises for ear training and sight-singing

Often times, church choirs are filled with members that LOVE to sing, but do not necessarily read music. Use these exercises to train singers in interval steps and leaps as well as music reading skills.

RETURNING TO THE ONE (MAJOR)

Practice intervals with this exercise.

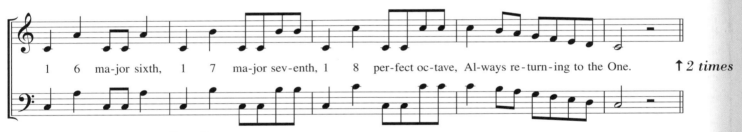

Piano Accompaniment • Page 99

RETURNING TO THE ONE (MINOR)

Sing the following interval drill in minor. Listen carefully for intonation.

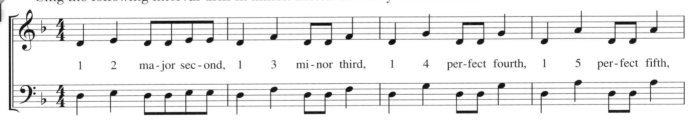

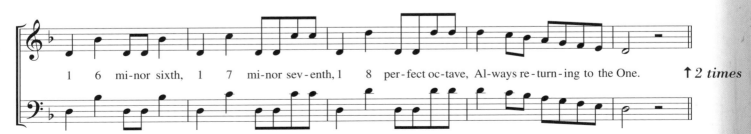

Piano Accompaniment • Page 101

SIGHT-SINGING IN C MAJOR IN 4/4

Every church choir will have a variety of sight-singing skill levels. The following concept can be applied to any four-part hymn in your hymnal. Have each section sight-read each line. Then put all parts together to practice your choral blend and intonation. Try a new one each week. Review pitches and durations before you begin each sight-singing exercise. You may choose to sing on numbers or a neutral syllable.

Have all singers read and sing Part 1. Depending on the level of your group, you may wish to begin with just the rhythms first. Then sing the pitches and rhythms. To gain confidence in sight-singing, give the starting pitch only. Let the singers read and sing on their own with no help from the piano, organ or the director.

Next, have all singers read and sing Part 2.

Next, have all singers read and sing Part 3.

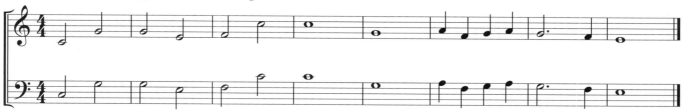

Then, have all singers read and sing Part 4.

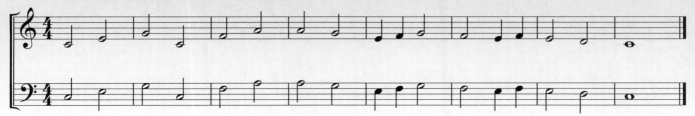

Next, ask singers to choose one of the four parts they have just sung. They may sing from one of the singer parts above, or you may distribute this combined score. Or assign Part 1 to the Altos, Part 2 to the Basses, Part 3 to Tenors, and Part 4 to the Sopranos. Then sing all four parts together, listening for balance and intonation between sections.

SIGHT-SINGING IN D MAJOR IN 3/4

Try this same concept in a new key and time signature. Remember to encourage singers to read on their own without the help of the piano or organ. This will develop independent singers that read music with confidence. Review pitches and durations before you begin each sight-singing exercise. You may choose to sing on numbers or a neutral syllable.

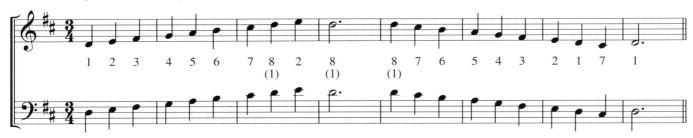

Have all singers read and sing Part 1. Depending on the level of your group, you may wish to begin with just the rhythms first. Then sing the pitches and rhythms.

Next, have all singers read and sing Part 2.

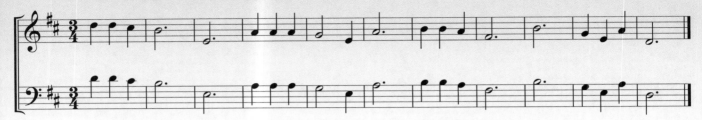

Next, have all singers read and sing Part 3.

Then, have all singers read and sing Part 4.

Next, ask singers to choose one of the four parts they have just sung. They may sing from one of the singer parts above, or you may distribute this combined score. Or assign Part 1 to the Tenors, Part 2 to the Basses, Part 3 to Altos, and Part 4 to the Sopranos. Then sing all four parts together. Tune and balance the sound of each 4-part chord.

CHAPTER 10
WHERE TWO OR MORE
ARE GATHERED
Activities for Fellowship and Camaraderie

Church choir rehearsals are not only a time to gather, warm-up, and prepare an anthem for worship service, but it is also a time for fellowship with members who share the same passion for spreading the Word through song. But how well do you know your neighbors in choir? These "getting to know you" activities can be used at choir retreats or at the end of every rehearsal to boost friendships among members and create a sense of unity within the group.

GETTING TO KNOW YOU

Pass out a blank sheet of paper (or create a reproducible) and have each choir member write something that others may not know about him/her. It may be job-related, a school they attended, a famous family member, a thrilling experience, an unknown talent, etc. Then turn it in to the director, making sure no one else sees it. Then at the end of each rehearsal, the director draws one from the stack and without revealing the contributor, reads it to the group. The group must then guess the member that contributed the tale. After the person is revealed, they may choose to expand the story.

THE HYMNBOOK CHOIR

Many congregations may have members that would love to share their time and talents with the choir, but for some reason have not been able to make the weekly rehearsal commitment. Offer them a chance to sing in the Hymnbook Choir. This choir meets 30 minutes prior to service and prepares a song from the church hymnal. The Hymnbook Choir can be an adjunct to your Adult Choir. Here are some ways to adapt a hymn for a choral performance in just 15-20 minutes of prep time.

1. Have the men, the women, or both sing one verse in unison.
2. Have the congregation join the choir on the final verse or chorus of a hymn.
3. Have the women sing one verse.
4. Have the men sing one verse.
5. Have the soprano and tenor sections sing a duet for one verse.
6. Have the tenors and basses sing the melody while the sopranos and altos sing the alto part.
7. Have one section of the choir sing the melody while the rest of the choir hums the other parts.
8. Have a soloist sing a verse or section.

A Hymnbook Choir not only allows members of the congregation to sing in a special presentation for the church service, but it also introduces them to the other choir members and shows them what fun can be in store for them if they join full time. Who knows? You may just get some new recruits.

TWO TRUTHS AND A LIE

Pass out a blank sheet of paper (or create a reproducible) and have each choir member write down three facts about themselves, one of them being a lie. At the end of each choir rehearsal, select a paper, read the three facts about the person to the group. Members must guess which one is untrue. Encourage members to be creative!

MAY THE BEST WORDS

Have each choir member submit his/her favorite quote, bible verse, song lyric, etc. Share them with the group at the end of the rehearsal and them post them on the choir room bulletin board.

BEACH BALL Q & A

On an inflated beach ball, write intriguing questions all over. At the end of each rehearsal, toss the ball to a choir member. They must answer the question touching their left thumb. Here are a few to get you started.

1. What do you think is your very best feature or characteristic?
2. What is your strongest talent?
3. If you could go anywhere in the world, where would you go?
4. What is your favorite sport to watch?
5. Which sport do you most enjoy actively participating in?
6. Can you recite all of the Ten Commandments from memory?
7. Which of all the prophets are you most eager to meet?
8. How many books did you read last year?
9. If you were called on to serve a mission, where would you least like to serve?
10. If you were called on to serve a mission, where would you most like to serve?
11. Are you creative in any way? If so, which way(s)?
12. Have you ever helped a stranger? If so, how?

GOD BE WITH YOU

Close each rehearsal with a benediction or sending song from your hymnal. This one has been adapted for musicians.

Text: Rankin, Alt. by J.D.
Music: Tomer

Piano Accompaniment • Page 103

"Music is the art of the prophets, the only art that can calm the agitations of the soul; it is one of the most magnificent and delightful presents God has given us." ~ Martin Luther

PRAISE GOD

31

YAHWEH

ALLELUIA, MANY VOICES AS ONE

Al - le - lu - ia, Al - le -

lu - ia

(Breathe over 4 counts.
Expand the rib cage.)

Al - le -

lu - ia, Al - le - lu - ia

CHURCH CHOIR WARM-UPS

HALLELUJAH VOWELS

1. Hallelujah.   2. He knows you.   3. He knows me too.   4. Hosanna.

Joy, joy, joy, joy, joy, joy. Let us sing a song of joy.

Joy, joy, joy, joy, joy, joy. Let us sing a song of joy.

Joy, joy, joy, joy, joy, joy. Let us sing a song of joy.

Joy, joy, joy, joy, joy, joy. Let us sing a song of joy.

Joy, joy, joy, joy, joy, joy. Let us sing a song of joy.

GOD LOVES YOU

loves you-hoo! Hey you! Who me? God loves you-hoo! Hey

you! Who me? God loves you-hoo! Hey you! Who me? God

loves you-hoo! Hey you! Who me? God loves you-hoo!

HOSANNA

SING WITH RESONANCE

RING THE BELLS

Ring the bells of Christ-mas, ring - a ding.

Ring the bells of Christ-mas, ring - a ding.

Ring the bells of Christ-mas, ring - a

ding. Ring the bells of Christ-mas, ring - a ding.

SING, SING, SING

ee, _____ sing eh, _____ sing ah. _____ Sing

ee, _____ sing eh, _____ sing ah. _____ Sing

ee, _____ sing eh, _____ sing ah. _____ Sing

SING ALLELUIA

Sing al - le - lu - ia

Sing al - le - lu - ia

Sing al - le - lu - ia

I KNOW THAT MY REDEEMER LIVES

Text from JOB 19:25

CHURCH CHOIR WARM-UPS

I know that my Re - deem - er lives!

I know that my Re - deem - er lives!

I know that my Re - deem - er lives!

HALLELUJAH, CHRIST HAS ARISEN

CHURCH CHOIR WARM-UPS

GOD IS GOOD

God is good__ all the time; All the time,__ God is good.

God is good__ all the time; All the time,__ God is good.

God is good__ all the time; All the time,__ God is good.

God is good __ all the time; All the time, __ God is good.

God is good __ all the time; All the time, __ God is good.

God is good __ all the time; All the time, __ God is good.

FOR UNTO US ARPEGGIOS

CHURCH CHOIR WARM-UPS

us_____ is born_____ a King.

For un - to us_____ is born_____ a King.

For un - to us_____ is born_____ a King.

I'LL SHOUT IT

MUSIC, SWEET MUSIC

AND THE NIGHT

OLD NOAH'S BOAT FLOATS

BRING A GIFT OF
SILK TO THE KING

ONE GOD, MANY MEMBERS

REJOICE

CHRIST STAR MERGING

WHAT'S WRONG WITH MY DIPHTHONG?

SOFT STILLNESS

I CAN DO ALL THINGS THROUGH CHRIST

Text from PHILIPPIANS 4:13

PRAISE HIM

Praise Him, Praise Him,   Praise ___ Him from whom all bless-ings   flow! _____

Praise Him, Praise Him,   Praise ___ Him from whom all bless-ings   flow! _____

Praise Him,   Praise Him,   Praise ___ Him from whom all bless-ings   flow! _____

Text from The Doxology

Praise Him, Praise Him, Praise ___ Him from whom all bless-ings flow! ___

Praise Him, Praise Him, Praise ___ Him from whom all bless-ings flow! ___

Praise Him, Praise Him, Praise ___ Him from whom all bless-ings flow! ___

SING PRAISE

ALLELUIA, AMEN

THE LORD IS MY SHEPHERD

The Lord Is my Shep-herd and I shall not want.

Text from PSALM 23

The Lord Is my Shep-herd and I shall not want.

The Lord Is my Shep-herd and I shall not want.

The Lord Is my Shep-herd and I shall not want.

LOVE IS PATIENT

Text from 1 CORINTHIANS 13:4

Love___ is___ pa - tient, love___ is___ kind.

Love___ is___ pa - tient, love___ is___ kind.

Love___ is___ pa - tient, love___ is___ kind.

CHURCH CHOIR WARM-UPS

WHERE TWO OR MORE
ARE GATHERED

Text from MATTHEW 18:20, Music: Music Alone Shall Live, Anonymous Canon

A ROUND OF AMENS

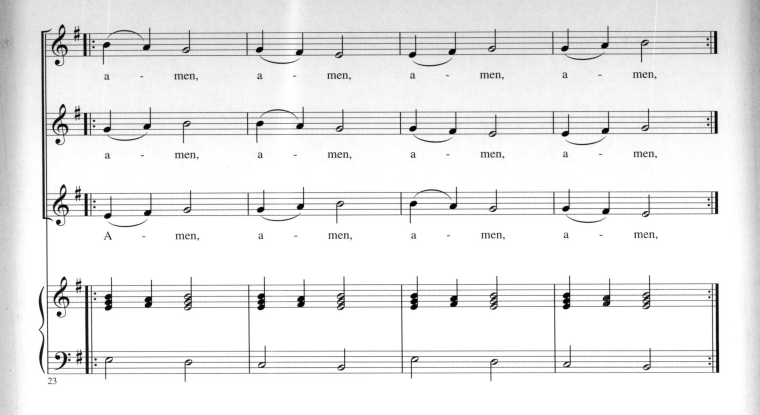

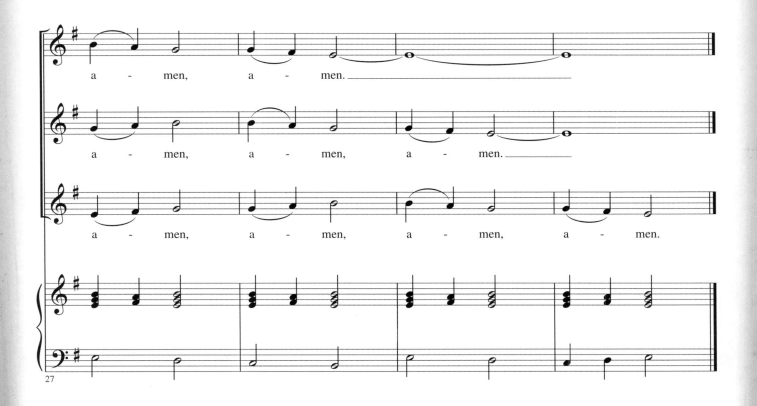

LET'S SING FOR JOY UNTO THE LORD

Text from PSALM 95:1, Music: Tallis' Canon

RETURNING TO
THE ONE (MAJOR)

RETURNING TO
THE ONE (MINOR)

CHURCH CHOIR WARM-UPS

GOD BE WITH YOU

Text: Rankin (1828 – 1904), Alt. by Day (2013)
Music: Tomer (1833 – 1896)

CHURCH CHOIR WARM-UPS

INDEX